Simple Pleasures for

BUSY MEN

DIMENSIONS

FOR LIVING

NASHVILLE

Simple Pleasures for Busy Men

ISBN 0-687-05540-7

Scripture quotations noted KJV are from the King James Version of the Bible.

Those noted NIV are taken from the Holy Bible: New International Version. Copyright © 1973, 1978, 1984 by the International Bible Society. Used by permission of Zondervan Bible Publishers.

Those noted NRSV are from the New Revised Standard Version Bible, copyright © 1989 by the Division of Christian Education of the National Council of the Churches of Christ in the United States of America, and are used by permission.

That noted TLB is from *The Living Bible*, copyright © 1971 by Tyndale House Publishers, Wheaton, IL. Used by permission.

96 97 98 99 00 01 02 03 04 05—10 9 8 7 6 5 4 3 2 1

MANUFACTURED IN THE UNITED STATES OF AMERICA

You show me the path of life.
In your presence there is
fullness of joy;
in your right hand
are pleasures forevermore.

—Psalm 16:11 NRSV

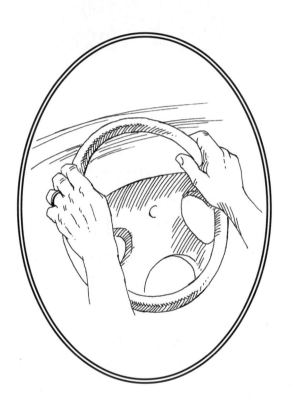

One

$\mathscr{A}$s you drive home from work, mentally prepare yourself to forget about your job and focus on your family's needs.

And ye shall return every man unto his family.

—Leviticus 25:10 KJV

Two

$\mathcal{M}$ake a homemade greeting card for someone you love.

Grace be to you, and peace, from God our Father, and from the Lord Jesus Christ.

—Ephesians 1:2 KJV

Three

*G*o for a walk or a run in the rain.

If ye walk in my statutes, and keep my commandments, and do them;
Then I will give you rain in due season, and the land shall yield her increase, and the trees of the field shall yield their fruit.

—Leviticus 26:3-4 KJV

Four

Have a snowball fight.

For as the rain cometh down, and the snow from heaven, and returneth not thither, but watereth the earth, and maketh it bring forth and bud, that it may give seed to the sower, and bread to the eater: So shall my word be that goeth forth out of my mouth: it shall not return unto me void, but it shall accomplish that which I please, and it shall prosper in the thing whereto I sent it.

—Isaiah 55:10-11 KJV

Five

$\mathscr{R}$ead aloud to your
wife, a friend, or a child;
then listen while that
person reads aloud
to you.

*My son, attend unto my wisdom, and bow
thine ear to my understanding: That thou
mayest regard discretion, and that thy lips
may keep knowledge.*

—Proverbs 5:1-2 KJV

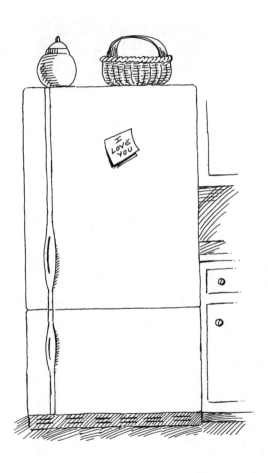

Six

Leave notes of appreciation and love around your house.

Many waters cannot quench love;
rivers cannot wash it away.

—Song of Solomon 8:7 NIV

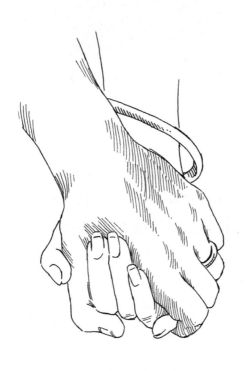

Seven

*T*ake a quiet walk-and-talk with your wife. Be sure to hold her hand.

Whoso findeth a wife findeth a good thing, and obtaineth favour of the Lord.

—Proverbs 18:22 KJV

Eight

*T*ake your children out for a Saturday morning excursion.

The just man walketh in his integrity: his children are blessed after him.

—Proverbs 20:7 KJV

Nine

*T*reat yourself or someone you love to a massage from a bona fide professional masseuse.

Though our outer nature is wasting away, our inner nature is being renewed day by day.

—2 Corinthians 4:16 NRSV

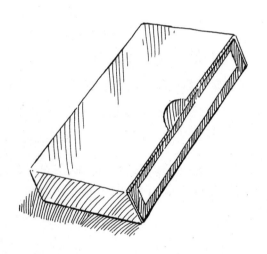

Ten

Put the children to bed early and watch a favorite video.

Return unto thy rest, O my soul; for the LORD hath dealt bountifully with thee.

—Psalm 116:7 KJV

Eleven

Bake some cookies.

The good person out of the good treasure of the heart produces good, . . . for it is out of the abundance of the heart that the mouth speaks.

—Luke 6:45 NRSV

Twelve

Celebrate the anniversary of a special "first" (you and your wife's first date, your first kiss, or the day you first met; a child's first steps or first time to ride a bike; your first day at work).

The LORD created me at the beginning of his work, the first of his acts of long ago.

—Proverbs 8:22 NRSV

Thirteen

For holidays or special occasions, buy a gift that can only be purchased in advance. It will show that you were thinking of the person.

The wisdom of the prudent is to give thought to their ways.

—Proverbs 14:8 NIV

Fourteen

Call someone you love during the middle of the day just to chat or say, "I love you."

Love never ends.

—1 Corinthians 13:8 NRSV

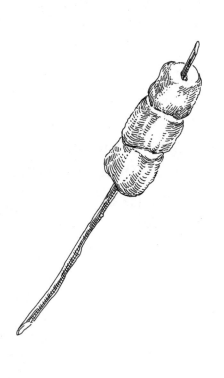

Fifteen

Roast marshmallows over a campfire at a nearby park.

*Thou crownest the year with thy goodness;
and thy paths drop fatness.*

—Psalm 65:11 KJV

Sixteen

*T*ake time to watch the sunset, or get up to watch the sunrise.

O LORD *my God, thou are very great; . . . Who coverest thyself with light as with a garment: who stretchest out the heavens like a curtain: Who layeth the beams of his chambers in the waters: who maketh the clouds his chariot: who walketh upon the wings of the wind.*

—Psalm 104:1-3 KJV

Seventeen

*A*lways kiss your wife hello and good-bye.

He that loveth his wife loveth himself.

—Ephesians 5:28

Eighteen

After breakfast, pray or study a devotional before you go to work.

*I will meditate also of all thy work,
and talk of thy doings.*

—Psalm 77:12 KJV

Nineteen

Play a romantic song (one of your wife's favorites or one that brings back special memories) and slow dance with her.

Let thy fountain be blessed: and rejoice with the wife of thy youth.

—Proverbs 5:18 KJV

Twenty

$\mathcal{D}$o some gardening or work in the yard.

You care for the land and water it; you enrich it abundantly. . . . For so you have ordained it.

—Psalm 65:9 NIV

Twenty-one

Write a poem.

My mouth shall speak of wisdom; and the meditation of my heart shall be of understanding.

—Psalm 49:3 KJV

Twenty-two

Go through your high school or college yearbook. Reflect on the hopes and dreams you had then. Think about the hopes and dreams you have now.

May our Lord Jesus Christ himself and God our Father, who loved us and by his grace gave us eternal encouragement and good hope, encourage your hearts and strengthen you in every good deed and word.

—2 Thessalonians 2:16-17 NIV

Twenty-three

Tell someone important
in your life why you
appreciate her or him.
Be specific.

You have a very special place in my heart.

—Philippians 1:17 TLB

Twenty-four

Go on a picnic and play Frisbee.

Therefore do not worry about tomorrow, for tomorrow will worry about itself.

—Matthew 6:34 NIV

Twenty-five

Cook dinner over your fireplace.

The *appetite of workers works for them; their hunger urges them on.*

—Proverbs 16:26 NRSV

Twenty-six

Clip a favorite comic strip and use it as a bookmark.

Even the world itself could not contain the books that should be written.

—John 21:25 KJV

Twenty-seven

$\mathcal{T}$ell your children the things you appreciate about their mother in front of her.

A word fitly spoken is like apples of gold in pictures of silver.

—Proverbs 25:11 KJV

Twenty-eight

Cook dinner with your kids. Clean up afterward.

Better is a dinner of vegetables where love is than a fatted ox and hatred with it.

—Proverbs 15:17 NRSV

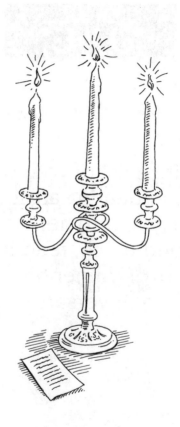

Twenty-nine

*W*rite a list of your wife's most endearing attributes and give it to her. As an added touch, read it to her over dinner on your anniversary.

Therefore shall a man leave his father and his mother, and shall cleave unto his wife: and they shall be one flesh.

—Genesis 2:24 KJV

Thirty

Rent a fun or fancy car for a special occasion or get-away weekend.

Come away to a deserted place all by yourselves and rest a while.

—Mark 6:31 NRSV